MAKE YOUR 1ST Cowls

LEISURE ARTS, INC. • Maumelle, Arkansas

Introduction

When a crocheter picks up the hook for the first time, they always have an idea of what it is they want to make; for some it is a scarf and for others it is a blanket. What if I told you that I believe neither is the best choice for the first item to make? I'm serious, a scarf might seem like the right choice because it is rather small widthwise but the amount of time it takes to get any suitable length often leaves the crocheter bored and lose interest. The same can be said about a blanket and we can add in the cost of the extra materials to make it. Those extra expenses can be hard to swallow as a new crocheter.

For these reasons and more, I believe that the cowl is the perfect first item for a new crocheter to make. The cowl is a highly fashionable and functional accessory that anybody can wear. Wide and chunky, slim and smooth, you see them on TV, in magazines, at the market, and on college campuses—everyone is wearing them. The cowl doesn't fall off your neck like a scarf; it can fit snug or be long and looped around your neck to have a flattering drape. It is the excellent layering piece for those of us who live in climates that have changing weather morning, noon, and night. The cowl can be dressed up or dressed down and is just an all around perfect addition to any wardrobe.

For crocheters, the cowl offers a blank canvas where they can experiment with stitches, textures and colors without having to make a HUGE time and material commitment. It is a great project to try out a new yarn or maybe use that one ball of "special yarn" you purchased on that family vacation 6 years ago. The possibilities that a cowl offers makes it the perfect first project.

MEET MARLY BIRD

I honestly believe anybody can crochet, it just takes a little patience and guidance to get there. I've been crocheting for over 20 years and teaching others how to crochet for 19 of those years. I love to teach others and watch the "a-ha!" moment in their eyes when they get it.

I want to present a series of books that hold your hand through the process of crochet—books that will walk you through step-by-step on how to make something.

Marly Bird™

Books that offer more than just instructions but also offer tips, tricks, suggestions for how to make it your own.

Books that you will pass down to your kids to show them how you learned to crochet.

"The cowl is a highly fashionable and functional accessory that anybody can wear."

Contents

What is so great about this book?

It's full of basic skill level cowls.

Need help?

Turn to Getting Started on page 4; it will help you jump right in and tackle your first one. Of course, I've given you my favorite hints and tips! Now, have fun creating your first cowl!

Linen Stitch.........................14

Chevron 18

Linen & V-Stitches.............22

Color Block Filet 26

Dreamy................................30

Blue Lace.............................34

Chic Chevron......................38

Triangle Mesh 42

Ribbed 46

Green Tea & Velvet............50

Are you looking for information about hooks or trying to understand the symbols?

Check out the General Instructions beginning on page 56. But, if you need a stitch refresher, you will find that in the Basic Crochet Stitches on pages 60-62.

Getting Started

This book is a great way to learn new stitches and use them to make a wonderful accessory. Take a moment to learn how to do basic stitches, then put your knowledge to work to make a simple piece like the Linen Stitch cowl or the Chevron cowl. Once you feel comfortable, you can begin to learn more intermediate stitches and then make the Dreamy cowl or the Blue Lace cowl. By the time you have made the cowls in this book, you will be ready to take on any crochet pattern or project.

Choosing yarn for your cowl is an exciting part of the crochet process. The possibilities are endless! Here are some of the top things you should consider when picking out the yarn you want to use.

WEIGHT

When following a pattern you often want to have a finished item that is similar to the sample. However, we know that there are times when you want to use a different yarn. Yes, you can do that. But, when you choose the new yarn, it is important that you pay attention to the weight of the yarn used in the sample versus the weight of your new yarn choice. The Craft Yarn Council (CYC) has made it easy for us crocheters to know the weights of yarn by assigning labels to them. We now have a standard to go by. On each of the patterns in this book, in the shopping list, you will find a symbol next to the yarn. That symbol indicates the CYC standard weight of the yarn used in the pattern. As long as you choose a yarn that has that same symbol or same weight, you should be good to go.

However, there are some of you who are daring and might be budding

designers who want to push the limits and use a completely different weight yarn than what the pattern calls for just to see what it will look like. DO IT! The results might surprise you! What was once big and bulky could end up sleek and sassy with a smaller weight yarn. That is one of the reasons I love making cowls, because making changes like this allow for us to really experiment with patterns and size.

A word of caution—if you change the weight of yarn for a project not only will the size of the cowl change (assuming you adjust the gauge to get what works best for the yarn you are using) but your yarn amounts will change. So be sure you have enough of the yarn you want to use.

FIBER

Just as the weight of the yarn is important, so too is the fiber content. Not all fibers are the same.

Each type of fiber has unique characteristics that must be taken into account when considering substitution (which is pretty much a pattern-by-pattern process).

Here are some examples:

Machine Washability

Mercerized merino, cotton and most acrylics are machine washable, but silk or pure wool are not.

Elasticity

This is the fiber's ability to stretch and contract, which affects an item's ability to regain its original shape. Animal fibers and some synthetics are stretchy, while plant fibers are not.

In general, the closer you stick to the recommended fiber type, the more predictable the results will be.

COLOR

Color can be very intimidating and sometimes challenging for a crafter. It is a difficult thing for me as well. Here is a little tip I have to help you put colors together. When I am working on a new pattern that has multiple colors, I always take a look at the different fabrics that are available. I look for color combinations that I like or that are on-trend. When I find one, I then find a yarn with the same or similar colors and go from there. Easy peasy, right?

The good news for you is that all the designs in this book either use only one color, a variegated yarn that does all the color changes for you, or many colors that complement one another like the Chic Chevron cowl or are different hues/shades of the same color like the Green Tea & Velvet cowl. If a particular color doesn't speak to you and you wish to change it, PLEASE, DO! You officially have my permission.

The best way to go about choosing a new color for your cowl is to pick a color you love, choose a variegated yarn with colors you love, or use the color wheel to help you choose complementary colors or different hues/shades of a color.

There are three types of colors—primary, secondary, and tertiary. Primary colors are red, blue, and yellow. Secondary colors are created by mixing two primary colors to create orange, green, and purple. Tertiary colors are

"I look for color combinations that I like or that are on trend. When I find one, I then find yarn with the same or similar colors and go from there."

Warm colors are happy and energetic while cool colors are soothing and peaceful. If you choose two colors on the color wheel that are directly opposite each other, they are complementary colors; which means you would have warm and cool colors that work well together.

created by mixing adjacent primary and secondary colors creating yellow-orange, yellow-green, blue-green, blue-purple, red-purple, and red-orange.

Now that we have explored colors, you can use several colors that all have the same temperature. Warm colors are yellow, orange, and red while cool colors are green, blue, and purple.

You can select 3 colors that are next to each other on the color wheel (such as red, red-purple, and purple). You can also create a palette with one family of hues: pastels, for example, or neutrals.

Another choice is to use a tonal mood and choose several shades of a single color like burgundy, red, and pink, for instance. Then add some black, white, or cream for more depth.

GAUGE

You can crochet for years without worrying about gauge, but as you expand your skills and really fine-tune your technique, you will want to follow patterns and recreate those items in both style and size. That is where the term gauge becomes very important.

Every crocheted fabric is made up of stitches and rows. Gauge is the number of stitches and rows it takes to make one square inch or one full repeat of the crocheted fabric. In any pattern, you will find the gauge the designer used to make that item. And, as long as you get the same number of stitches and the same number of rows to equal the measurement as written in the pattern, then you are sure to get the same size as the designer intended.

Gauge isn't always important, such as when you're making a scarf, an afghan, a bag, or anything else for which a precise size isn't essential. But when size does matter, the right or wrong gauge can make or break the finished piece.

Things that affect gauge include the yarn, the hook size and brand, and the stitch pattern you use to make your cowl. Yarns of different weights produce different gauges.

". . . when size does matter, the right or wrong gauge can make or break the finished piece."

A bulkier yarn produces a larger stitch, for example, while a finer yarn produces a smaller stitch. Hooks and stitch size—the same yarn crocheted on different size hooks will have different gauges; the same can be said of different brands of hooks. Because you make a stitch by wrapping yarn around the hook, the size (circumference) of the hook determines the size of the stitch.

As for the brand, different brands of hooks are styled to have different points, throats and shafts and as a result, a crocheter will crochet differently with different hooks. Therefore, it is important that when your gauge swatch is complete and you get a yarn and hook combination that works for you, be sure to stick with that exact hook throughout the project.

Gauge Swatches

Just as it is important to use the same hook you plan on using for your project. It is important that you use the same yarn for your gauge swatch as for your project, not the same brand in a different color. Different dyes can affect how a specific yarn crochets up, and believe it or not, a yarn in one color can give you a different gauge from the same yarn in a different color.

To make your swatch, follow these steps:

1. Chain the stitch multiple for the stitch pattern you are going to use. Guesstimate about how many multiples you need to yield a fabric that is at least 5" (12.75 cm) wide.
2. Work in the stitch pattern for the number of rows of the row pattern repeat, then enough more rows to yield 5" (12.75 cm) tall.
3. Finish off, cut the strand of yarn, leaving an 8" (20.5 cm) tail.

4. Block the swatch in the same manner you plan to use for your finished project.

Measure Gauge Swatch

To measure your swatch, smooth it out on a flat surface. Pin the edges down if they're curling in—be careful not to stretch your swatch—and follow these steps:

1. Lay a ruler along a row of stitches and mark the beginning and end of 4" (10 cm) with straight pins.
2. Note the number of stitches or stitch pattern repeats in 4" (10 cm), fractions and all.
3. Lay your ruler along a vertical line of stitches, aligning the bottom of the ruler with the bottom of a stitch, and put a straight pin in to show where the first stitch begins. Place another straight pin 4" (10 cm) up.
4. Count the rows between the pins, fractions and all, and note the number of rows.

Oh my, the dreaded gauge swatch! When you decide to create a project that needs to fit, that's the time for finding the importance of a gauge swatch. Gauge swatches will save you time, money and tears with a completed design that fits properly and that you will love.

You now know the number of stitches or stitch pattern repeats, as well as the row or row pattern repeats you get with that yarn and that hook over 4" (10 cm). Check to see if those measurements are the same as what the pattern indicates you need. If it is spot on, lucky you!

If it is off, here is what you do. If the stitches or stitch pattern repeats are too many, then your stitches are too small and you need to go up a hook size. If the stitches or stitch pattern repeat are too few, then your stitches are too big and you need to go down a hook size. Easy as that. But, work another swatch to be sure using the different size hook will work.

Blocking

For any finished item that you plan on wearing and washing at some point, you want to actually wash the swatch. Treat the swatch as you would the finished item. Use soap, put it in the washer (if it is machine washable) and let it dry. Doing so will help you see how the fabric will behave after washing. Does it hold together? Does it pill? Does it stretch? All of these things are important to know before you spend your time using that yarn to make a full-size item.

Those are the benefits of washing your swatch, but what about the blocking part? First, did you know that the given gauge in a pattern is the blocked gauge (unless noted differently)? That means, it is entirely possible to have a pre-blocked gauge of 3 stitch pattern repeats = 4" (10 cm) but after blocking the measurement can increase to 2 stitch pattern repeats = 4" (10 cm). Over the course of a full project, that is a HUGE difference. Therefore, it is imperative that you know what the blocked gauge is of your swatch.

Now, for the most part, wet blocking acrylic yarn doesn't really do

Here are some basic crochet supplies—yarn, crochet hooks, yarn needles, ruler, and stitch markers.

anything to change it, but when you are using a wool, like Chic Sheep by Marly Bird™, blocking is very important. Specifically, I suggest wet blocking.

Just as I mentioned above, you want to wash your swatch. For wool, I suggest hand-washing the finished swatch in your sink and use a wool wash. When you do this you are giving that yarn a spa treatment. The yarn has been handled, tugged, pulled, crocheted and really just needs a chance to relax and let the fibers settle into place. Not only will the yarn really show its true beauty when cleaned but it will block even more beautifully.

After the swatch has had a good wash, follow these steps to block it out.

1. Get as much water out of your swatch as you can without stretching or wringing it out. ***Note:*** When you lift the piece out of the sink, lift it out in both hands, making sure not to let any part of it stretch down.
2. Without stretching the piece, spread it out on the towel and fold the ends of the towel over it; then gently and loosely roll up the towel to absorb more water.
3. Gently lay your piece out on the blocking board.

BLOCKING TIP:
I like to use the cardboard cutting boards from the fabric section of the big box store. The grid lines on the board make it easy to measure out and block my swatch or my finished piece.

***Note:* Before you use it, be sure to use a damp paper towel and wipe it down to get rid of any extra ink!**

4. Spread your piece out using the measurements of the piece as a guide.
5. Using straight pins, pin and smooth all pieces.
6. Allow the piece to air dry. Keep the piece out of the sun as that may cause discoloration. If you're in a hurry, you can get your piece to dry in a matter of hours by placing a fan in front of it.

The last thing to do after the swatch has been blocked is to unpin it from the blocking board, let it rest for a couple minutes then measure it for the gauge.

Hints & Tips

Do you get wonky edges?

Place a locking stitch marker in the turning chain or first stitch of the row to help you know where the last stitch of that row is on the following row. Then with each subsequent row, move that marker up to help you keep track. This is especially helpful for stitch patterns that count the turning chain as a stitch.

Are chevron stitches giving you trouble?

When I do chevrons I think of them as peaks and valleys. When you get to a peak of a chevron you have to do an increase (put more than one stitch into a stitch/space indicated), when you are in the valley you have to do a decrease (eliminate a stitch by skipping a stitch or working two stitches together). As long as I maintain the increase at the peaks and decreases in the valleys, I am sure to get perfect chevrons.

I love this cowl but I want it to be longer/shorter.

That is an easy one! Should you like the look of a particular cowl, like the Ribbed cowl, but you want it to be longer, all you have to do is increase the number of stitch multiples across. Sticking with this cowl as the example, the pattern has you chain 102 and after the first row you have 100 stitches. That means if we want to double the length of the cowl we would have to chain 202 to get a total of 200 stitches (those extra 2 chains are on the turning chain and do not get doubled).

For any of the other patterns, you can double the chains as I did or find the stitch multiple and make changes to the chain amount that coincides with the stitch multiple.

Love the stitch pattern but not the variegated yarn?

Not a problem, get a completely different look by choosing a solid color yarn to make the cowl. Or maybe choose to make a cowl in stripes instead of a solid. Have fun with these cowls! They are your blank canvases!

Can I make this in the round?

The short answer is yes; however, there are changes that need to be made with the actual stitch patterns to alter a pattern from being worked in rows to in rounds. If you are comfortable making these changes then yes, you can change the pattern. But, if you are not familiar with how to do that, I suggest working the cowl patterns as written.

I hate weaving in ends... what can I do?

Well, first, know that you are not alone with that opinion. Not many crocheters I know enjoy weaving in ends. BUT, it is a necessary evil. I am not a fan of just crocheting over ends so please do not do that. Take the time to properly weave in your ends.

Or turn the tails of your yarn into a fashion statement by making them fringe! Fringe is HOT right now and would absolutely turn your fashionable piece into something very haute couture. Talk about making lemonade out of lemons!

Oh No, there is a knot in my yarn!

Ya, it happens. You will be crocheting along when all of a sudden there is a knot in the yarn from the manufacturer. Don't panic, it is just a simple little knot. The first thing I want to tell you is this, are you listening? No, really, are you listening? Okay, here it is...DO NOT

"Have fun with these cowls! They are your blank canvases!"

CROCHET OVER THE KNOT! That's right, you want to go ahead and back up a few stitches, leave yourself at least 4-6" (10-15 cm) of length, cut that yarn with the knot, then again leaving a 4-6" (10-15 cm) tail of the yarn, rejoin the yarn as you would if you were changing colors and carry on.

This makes for more ends to weave in, yes. But it also means you will have a better finished piece that doesn't have knots in the middle of the fabric. Plus, you have no idea if those knots are secure and the last thing you want is to have the knot come undone as you are wearing your cowl, right?

I made changes but I can't remember what I did!

This happens to me all the time; I get excited about a project or pattern and just want to work on it. Like many of you, I lie to myself by saying that I will remember what I did, then days go by, I pick up my pattern and I have no idea what I am doing. Learn from my mistakes. The best

Add that something EXTRA!

Sometimes you can finish a piece and think that it needs a little something . . . extra. Maybe that extra is fringe or a pom-pom or tassels. Whatever that extra is for you, I encourage you to do it. Those little finishing touches can really make a piece.

If it interests you, I suggest adding small pom-poms along the edge of the Chevron cowl. Or make the cowl into a scarf and add pom-poms to the points on either end.

piece of advice I can offer is to take notes as you are working on a project. If a pen and paper is your jam, great! Be sure to have a notebook next to you as you work on your cowl and jot down notes (what yarn are you using, what hook size and brand, what was your gauge, what is the title of the book and the page number of the pattern you are using, etc.).

If you are more tech savvy, then pop open an app that you can keep notes in and use that. I know that every phone, pad, tablet or whatnot has their own so I am not going to recommend any here.

The bottom line is this, taking notes is very important when you are working on any pattern. It is a place that you can keep track of the details of your pattern or even keep a tally of the number of repeats or rows you have completed. But notes are especially important if you're making changes to a pattern.

Can I add buttons?

Sure! Better yet, you can just add buttons and no buttonholes! For pieces like the Linen & V-Stitches cowl, once you seam it together, you can add decorative buttons to one of the linen stitch sections to make it look like it is actually buttoned. It could add a nice detail without a lot of extra work.

Should you want to add buttons and buttonholes to one of the cowls for closure instead of seaming, you can absolutely do that. If the cowl doesn't have a very open fabric that can be used as buttonholes, you will have to add extra rows of stitches.

1. Place locking stitch markers at each spot where you want a buttonhole (make sure they are evenly spaced). Single crochet to the marker, ★ chain 1 (or more), skip 1 stitch (or more; skip the same number of stitches as you made in your chain), single crochet to next marker; repeat from ★ until all buttonholes are complete, then work to end of row.
2. On the next row, work one single crochet into the chain space for each stitch skipped.

You now have buttonholes. Sew the actual buttons to the other side of the cowl and close.

"The bottom line is this, taking notes is very important when you are working on any pattern . . . notes are especially important if you're making changes to a pattern."

Projects

Linen Stitch

BASIC

Finished Size:

8¼" wide x 40" circumference
(21 cm x 101.5 cm)

GAUGE INFORMATION

In pattern,
15 sts and 14 rows = 4" (10 cm)

Gauge Swatch: 4" (10 cm) square

Ch 16.

Work same as Cowl for 14 rows: 15 sts.

Finish off.

COWL

Ch 32.

Row 1: Sc in second ch from hook and in each ch across: 31 sc.

Row 2 (Right side)**:** Ch 1, turn; sc in first sc, (dc in next sc, sc in next sc) across.

Note: Loop a short piece of yarn around any stitch to mark Row 2 as **right** side.

Row 3: Ch 3 **(counts as first dc)**, turn; (sc in next dc, dc in next sc) across.

Row 4: Ch 1, turn; sc in first dc, (dc in next sc, sc in next dc) across.

Shopping List

Yarn (Medium Weight)

MEDIUM 4

[4 ounces, 210 yards (113 grams, 193 meters) per skein]:

☐ 2 skeins

Crochet Hook

☐ Size I (5.5 mm)
or size needed for gauge

Additional Supplies

☐ Yarn needle

Repeat Rows 3 and 4 for pattern until Cowl measures approximately 39¾" (101 cm) from beginning ch, ending by working Row 4.

Last Row: Ch 1, turn; sc in each st across; finish off leaving a long end for sewing.

With **right** side together, matching sc on last row with beginning ch, whipstitch seam *(Fig. 6, page 59)*.

Chevron

BASIC

Finished Size:
7" wide x 39½" circumference
(18 cm x 100.5 cm)

GAUGE INFORMATION

In pattern, two repeats (27 sts)
and 6 rows = 3½" (9 cm)

Gauge Swatch:
7" wide x 3½" high (18 cm x 9 cm)
Work same as Cowl for 6 rows: 26 dc and one ch-1 sp.

STITCH GUIDE

DOUBLE CROCHET 3 TOGETHER
(abbreviated dc3tog)
(uses next 3 sts)
★ YO, insert hook in **next** st, YO and pull up a loop, YO and draw through 2 loops on hook; repeat from ★ 2 times **more**, YO and draw through all 4 loops on hook (**counts as one dc**).

COWL

Ch 30.

Row 1: Dc in fourth ch from hook **(3 skipped chs count as first dc)** and in next 4 chs, dc3tog, dc in next 5 chs, (dc, ch 1, dc) in next ch, dc in next 5 chs, dc3tog, dc in next 4 chs, 2 dc in last ch: 26 dc and one ch-1 sp.

Row 2 (Right side)**:** Ch 3 **(counts as first dc, now and throughout)**, turn; working in Back Loops Only ***(Fig. 1, page 58)***, dc in first 5 dc, dc3tog, dc in next 5 dc, (dc, ch 1, dc) in next ch, dc in next 5 dc, dc3tog, dc in next 4 dc, 2 dc in last dc.

Note: Loop a short piece of yarn around any stitch to mark Row 2 as **right** side.

Row 3: Ch 3, turn; working in Back Loops Only, dc in first 5 dc, dc3tog, dc in next 5 dc, (dc, ch 1, dc) in next ch, dc in next 5 dc, dc3tog, dc in next 4 dc, 2 dc in last dc.

Repeat Row 3 for pattern until Cowl measures approximately 39½" (100.5 cm) from beginning ch, ending by working a **right** side row.

Finish off leaving a long end for sewing.

With **right** side together, matching sts on last row with beginning ch, whipstitch seam ***(Fig. 6, page 59)*** working in Back Loops Only on last row.

Shopping List

Yarn (Medium Weight)
MEDIUM 4

[10 ounces, 482 yards
(283 grams, 440 meters)
per skein]:
☐ 225 yards (206 meters)

Crochet Hook

☐ Size I (5.5 mm)
or size needed for gauge

Additional Supplies

☐ Yarn needle

Linen & V-Stitches

BASIC

Shopping List

Yarn (Medium Weight)

MEDIUM 4

[3.5 ounces, 186 yards (100 grams, 170 meters) per skein]:

☐ 2 skeins

Crochet Hook

☐ Size I (5.5 mm) **or** size needed for gauge

Additional Supplies

☐ Yarn needle

Finished Size:

11" wide x 40½" circumference (28 cm x 103 cm)

GAUGE INFORMATION

In V-St pattern, 4 V-sts = 3" (7.5 cm); 11 rows = 5¾" (14.5 cm)

Gauge Swatch: 3½" wide x 3" high (9 cm x 7.5 cm)

Ch 12.

Work same as Cowl for 7 rows: 4 V-Sts.

Finish off.

STITCH GUIDE

V-STITCH ***(abbreviated V-St)*** (uses one st or sp)

(Dc, ch 1, dc) in st or sp indicated.

COWL

Ch 32.

Row 1 (Right side)**:** Sc in second ch from hook and in each ch across: 31 sc.

Note: Loop a short piece of yarn around any stitch to mark Row 1 as **right** side.

Row 2: Ch 1, turn; sc in first sc, (dc in next sc, sc in next sc) across.

Row 3: Ch 3 **(counts as first dc, now and throughout)**, turn; (sc in next dc, dc in next sc) across.

Row 4: Ch 1, turn; sc in first dc, (dc in next sc, sc in next dc) across.

Row 5: Ch 3, turn; skip first 2 sts, work V-St in next sc, ★ skip next dc, work V-St in next sc; repeat from ★ across to last 2 sts, skip next dc, dc in last sc: 14 V-Sts.

Rows 6-15: Ch 3, turn; work V-St in each V-St (ch-1 sp) across, dc in last dc.

Row 16: Ch 1, turn; sc in first 2 dc, (skip next ch, sc in next 2 dc) across to last ch-1 sp, sc in last ch-1 sp and in last 2 dc: 31 sc.

Row 17: Ch 1, turn; sc in first sc, (dc in next sc, sc in next sc) across.

Row 18: Ch 3, turn; (sc in next dc, dc in next sc) across.

Row 19: Ch 1, turn; sc in first dc, (dc in next sc, sc in next dc) across.

Repeat Rows 5-19 for pattern until Cowl measures approximately 40½" (103 cm) from beginning ch, ending by working Row 15.

Finish off leaving a long end for sewing.

With **right** side together, matching sts on last row with beginning ch, whipstitch seam ***(Fig. 6, page 59)***.

Color Block Filet

BASIC

Shopping List

Yarn (Medium Weight)

MEDIUM 4

[5 ounces, 256 yards (141 grams, 234 meters) per skein]:

- ☐ Grey - 100 yards (91.5 meters)
- ☐ White - 100 yards (91.5 meters)
- ☐ Green - 100 yards (91.5 meters)

[4 ounces, 212 yards (113 grams, 194 meters) per skein]:

- ☐ Lt Grey - 100 yards (91.5 meters)

Crochet Hook

- ☐ Size I (5.5 mm) **or** size needed for gauge

Additional Supplies

- ☐ Yarn needle

Finished Size:
10¾" wide x 39" circumference (27.5 cm x 99 cm)

GAUGE INFORMATION

In pattern,
one repeat (12 sts) = 3" (7.5 cm);
10 rows = 4" (10 cm)

Gauge Swatch: 6¼" wide x 4" high (16 cm x 10 cm)

Ch 27.

Work same as Cowl for 10 rows: 19 dc and 6 ch-1 sps.

Finish off.

COWL

With Grey, ch 159.

Row 1 (Right side)**:** Dc in fourth ch from hook **(3 skipped chs count as first dc)** and in next 5 chs, ch 1, skip next ch, (dc in next ch, ch 1, skip next ch) twice, ★ dc in next 7 chs, ch 1, skip next ch, (dc in next ch, ch 1, skip next ch) twice; repeat from ★ across to last ch, dc in last ch: 118 dc and 39 chs.

Note: Loop a short piece of yarn around any stitch to mark Row 1 as **right** side.

Row 2: Ch 4 **(counts as first dc plus ch 1, now and throughout)**, turn; skip next ch, (dc in next dc, ch 1, skip next ch) twice, dc in next 7 dc, ★ ch 1, skip next ch, (dc in next dc, ch 1, skip next ch) twice, dc in next 7 dc; repeat from ★ across.

Row 3: Ch 3 **(counts as first dc, now and throughout)**, turn; dc in next 6 dc, ch 1, skip next ch, (dc in next dc, ch 1, skip next ch) twice, ★ dc in next 7 dc, ch 1, skip next ch, (dc in next dc, ch 1, skip next ch) twice; repeat from ★ across to last dc, dc in last dc; finish off.

Row 4: With **wrong** side facing, join Lt Grey with slip st in first dc; ch 3, ★ (dc in next ch and in next dc) 3 times, (ch 1, skip next dc, dc in next dc) 3 times; repeat from ★ across.

Row 5: Ch 4, turn; skip next ch, (dc in next dc, ch 1, skip next ch) twice, dc in next 7 dc, ★ ch 1, skip next ch, (dc in next dc, ch 1, skip next ch) twice, dc in next 7 dc; repeat from ★ across.

Row 6: Ch 3, turn; dc in next 6 dc, ch 1, skip next ch, (dc in next dc, ch 1, skip next ch) twice, ★ dc in next 7 dc, ch 1, skip next ch, (dc in next dc, ch 1, skip next ch) twice; repeat from ★ across to last dc, dc in last dc; finish off.

Rows 7-9: With **right** side facing and using White, repeat Rows 4-6.

Rows 10-12: With Green, repeat Rows 4-6.

Rows 13-15: With **right** side facing and using Grey, repeat Rows 4-6.

Rows 16-27: Repeat Rows 4-15; at end of Row 27, finish off leaving a long end for sewing.

With **right** side facing, sew ends of rows together using mattress stitch ***(Figs. 5a & b, page 59)***.

Dreamy

BASIC

Shopping List

Yarn (Bulky Weight)

BULKY 5

[8.8 ounces, 466 yards (250 grams, 426 meters) per skein]:

☐ 1 skein

Crochet Hook

☐ Size I (5.5 mm) **or** size needed for gauge

Additional Supplies

☐ Yarn needle

Finished Size:

15" wide x 44" circumference (38 cm x 112 cm)

GAUGE INFORMATION

In pattern, 11 sts = 4" (10 cm); 6 rows (Rows 4-9) = 2¾" (7 cm)

Gauge Swatch: 4" wide x 4½" high (10 cm x 11.5 cm)

Ch 12.

Work same as Cowl for 9 rows: 11 hdc.

Finish off.

STITCH GUIDE

PUFF STITCH ***(abbreviated Puff St)*** (uses one sc)

★ YO, insert hook in sc indicated, YO and pull up a loop; repeat from ★ 2 times **more**, YO and draw through 6 loops on hook, YO and draw through remaining 2 loops on hook.

COWL

Ch 122.

Row 1 (Right side)**:** Sc in second ch from hook and in each ch across: 121 sc.

Note: Loop a short piece of yarn around any stitch to mark Row 1 as **right** side.

Row 2: Ch 1, turn; hdc in Back Loop Only of each sc across ***(Fig. 1, page 58)***.

Row 3: Ch 1, turn; hdc in Front Loop Only of each hdc across ***(Fig. 1, page 58)***.

Row 4: Ch 1, turn; sc in both loops of each hdc across.

Row 5: Ch 1, turn; hdc in first sc, ch 1, ★ skip next sc, work Puff St in next sc, ch 1; repeat from ★ across to last 2 sc, skip next sc, hdc in last sc: 59 Puff Sts, 2 hdc, and 60 chs.

Row 6: Ch 1, turn; sc in each st and in each ch across: 121 sc.

Row 7: Ch 1, turn; hdc in Back Loop Only of each sc across.

Rows 8 and 9: Ch 1, turn; hdc in Front Loop Only of each hdc across.

Rows 10-31: Repeat Rows 4-9, 3 times; then repeat Rows 4-7 once **more**.

Row 32: Ch 1, turn; hdc in Front Loop Only of each hdc across.

Row 33: Ch 1, turn; sc in both loops of each hdc across; finish off leaving a long end for sewing.

With **right** side facing, sew ends of rows together using mattress stitch ***(Figs. 5a & b, page 59)***.

Blue Lace

BASIC

Shopping List

Yarn (Medium Weight)

MEDIUM 4

[3.5 ounces, 186 yards (100 grams, 170 meters) per skein]:

☐ 1 skein

Crochet Hook

☐ Size I (5.5 mm) **or** size needed for gauge

Additional Supplies

☐ Yarn needle

Finished Size: 8¼" wide x 28" circumference (21 cm x 71 cm)

GAUGE INFORMATION

In pattern, 2 repeats = 3¾" (9.5 cm); 10 rows (Rows 3-12) = 4½" (11.5 cm)

Gauge Swatch: 7¾" wide x 5¼" high (19.75 cm x 13.25 cm)

Work same as Cowl through Row 12: 31 sc.

STITCH GUIDE

CLUSTER (uses one st)

★ YO, insert hook in st indicated, YO and pull up a loop, YO and draw through 2 loops on hook; repeat from ★ once **more**, YO and draw through all 3 loops on hook.

COWL

Ch 32.

Row 1: Sc in second ch from hook and in next 2 chs, ch 2, ★ skip next ch, sc in next 5 chs, ch 2; repeat from ★ across to last 4 chs, skip next ch, sc in last 3 chs: 26 sc and 5 ch-2 sps.

Row 2 (Right side)**:** Ch 1, turn; sc in each sc and in each ch-2 sp across: 31 sc.

Note: Loop a short piece of yarn around any stitch to mark Row 2 as **right** side.

Row 3: Ch 1, turn; sc in first sc, (dc in next sc, sc in next sc) across.

Row 4: Ch 3 **(counts as first dc, now and throughout)**, turn; (sc in next dc, dc in next sc) across.

Row 5: Ch 1, turn; sc in first dc, (dc in next sc, sc in next dc) across.

Row 6: Ch 2, turn; dc in first sc **(counts as first Cluster)**, ch 2, work Cluster in same sc, skip next 2 sts, sc in next dc, ★ skip next 3 sts, work Cluster in next dc, (ch 2, work Cluster in same dc) twice, skip next 3 sts, sc in next dc; repeat from ★ 2 times **more**, skip next 2 sts, work (Cluster, ch 2, Cluster) in last sc: 13 Clusters, 4 sc, and 8 ch-2 sps.

Row 7: Ch 1, turn; sc in top of first Cluster, ★ ch 3, skip next ch-2 sp and next Cluster, dc in next sc, ch 3, skip next Cluster and next ch-2 sp, sc in top of next Cluster; repeat from ★ across: 9 sts and 8 ch-3 sps.

Row 8: Ch 1, turn; sc in first sc, ★ skip next ch-3 sp, work Cluster in next dc, (ch 2, work Cluster in same dc) twice, skip next ch-3 sp, sc in next sc; repeat from ★ across: 12 Clusters, 5 sc, and 8 ch-2 sps.

Row 9: Ch 6 **(counts as first dc plus ch 3)**, turn; skip next Cluster and next ch-2 sp, sc in top of next Cluster, ch 3, skip next ch-2 sp and next Cluster, dc in next sc, ★ ch 3, skip next Cluster and next ch-2 sp, sc in top of next Cluster, ch 3, skip next ch-2 sp and next Cluster, dc in next sc; repeat from ★ across: 9 sts and 8 ch-3 sps.

Row 10: Ch 2, turn; dc in first dc **(counts as first Cluster)**, ch 2, work Cluster in same dc, skip next ch-3 sp, sc in next sc, ★ skip next ch-3 sp, work Cluster in next dc, (ch 2, work Cluster in same dc) twice, skip next ch-3 sp, sc in next sc; repeat from ★ 2 times **more**, skip next ch-3 sp, work (Cluster, ch 2, Cluster) in last dc: 13 Clusters, 4 sc, and 8 ch-2 sps.

Row 11: Repeat Row 7: 9 sts and 8 ch-3 sps.

Row 12: Ch 1, turn; sc in first sc, 2 sc in next ch-3 sp, sc in next dc, ★ 3 sc in next ch-3 sp, sc in next sc, 3 sc in next ch-3 sp, sc in next dc; repeat from ★ 2 times **more**, 2 sc in next ch-3 sp, sc in last sc: 31 sc.

Rows 13-62: Repeat Rows 3-12, 5 times; at end of Row 62, finish off leaving a long end for sewing.

With **right** side together, matching sts on Row 62 with beginning ch, whipstitch seam *(Fig. 6, page 59)*.

Trim

With **right** side facing, join yarn with slip st in seam on either edge; ch 1, working in ends of rows from **left** to **right**, work reverse sc in each row around *(Figs. 7a-d, page 59)*; join with slip st to first st, finish off.

Repeat Trim on opposite edge of Cowl.

Chic Chevron

BASIC

Shopping List

Yarn (Medium Weight)

MEDIUM 4

[3.5 ounces, 186 yards (100 grams, 170 meters) per skein]:

- ☐ Mint - 2 skeins
- ☐ White - 1 skein
- ☐ Red - 1 skein

Crochet Hook

- ☐ Size I (5.5 mm) **or** size needed for gauge

Additional Supplies

- ☐ Yarn needle

Finished Size:
9¾" wide x 41" circumference (25 cm x 104 cm)

GAUGE INFORMATION

In pattern,
one repeat = 4¼" wide (10.75 cm);
7 rows = 4" (10 cm)

Gauge Swatch: 8¾" wide x 3½" high (22.25 cm x 9 cm)

Work same as Cowl for 6 rows: 46 sts and 2 ch-3 sps.

STITCH GUIDE

CLUSTER (uses one st or sp)
★ YO, insert hook in st or sp indicated, YO and pull up a loop, YO and draw through 2 loops on hook; repeat from ★ 2 times **more**, YO and draw through all 4 loops on hook.

COWL

With White, ch 49.

Row 1 (Right side)**:** Sc in second ch from hook and in each ch across; changing to Mint in last sc *(Fig. 2a, page 58)*, do **not** cut White: 48 sc.

Note: Loop a short piece of yarn around any stitch to mark Row 1 as **right** side.

Row 2: Ch 3 **(counts as first dc, now and throughout)**, turn; skip first 3 sc, (3 dc in next sc, skip next 2 sc) 3 times, (3 dc, ch 3, 3 dc) in next sc, (skip next 2 sc, 3 dc in next sc) twice, skip next 2 sc, work Cluster in next sc, skip next 4 sc, work Cluster in next sc, skip next 2 sc, (3 dc in next sc, skip next 2 sc) twice, (3 dc, ch 3, 3 dc) in next sc, skip next 2 sc, (3 dc in next sc, skip next 2 sc) 3 times, dc in last sc changing to Red *(Fig. 2b, page 58)*; do **not** cut Mint: 46 sts and 2 ch-3 sps.

Dropped yarns will be carried **loosely** at end of each row.

Row 3: Ch 3, turn; skip next 3 dc, [3 dc in sp **before** next dc *(Fig. 3, page 58)*, skip next 3 dc] 3 times, (3 dc, ch 3, 3 dc) in next ch-3 sp, (skip next 3 dc, 3 dc in sp **before** next dc) twice, skip next 3 dc, work Cluster in sp **before** next Cluster, skip next 2 Clusters, work Cluster in sp **before** next dc, skip next 3 dc, (3 dc in sp **before** next dc, skip next 3 dc) twice, (3 dc, ch 3, 3 dc) in next ch-3 sp, skip next 3 dc, (3 dc in sp **before** next dc, skip next 3 dc) 3 times, dc in last dc changing to White.

Row 4: Ch 3, turn; skip next 3 dc, (3 dc in sp **before** next dc, skip next 3 dc) 3 times, (3 dc, ch 3, 3 dc) in next ch-3 sp, (skip next 3 dc, 3 dc in sp **before** next dc) twice, skip next 3 dc, work Cluster in sp **before** next Cluster, skip next 2 Clusters, work Cluster in sp **before** next dc, skip next 3 dc, (3 dc in sp **before** next dc, skip next 3 dc) twice, (3 dc, ch 3, 3 dc) in next ch-3 sp, skip next 3 dc, (3 dc in sp **before** next dc, skip next 3 dc) 3 times, dc in last dc changing to Mint.

Row 5: Ch 3, turn; skip next 3 dc, (3 dc in sp **before** next dc, skip next 3 dc) 3 times, (3 dc, ch 3, 3 dc) in next ch-3 sp, (skip next 3 dc, 3 dc in sp **before** next dc) twice, skip next 3 dc, work Cluster in sp **before** next Cluster, skip next 2 Clusters, work Cluster in sp **before** next dc, skip next 3 dc, (3 dc in sp **before** next dc, skip next 3 dc) twice, (3 dc, ch 3, 3 dc) in next ch-3 sp, skip next 3 dc, (3 dc in sp **before** next dc, skip next 3 dc) 3 times, dc in last dc changing to Red.

Repeat Rows 3-5 for pattern until Cowl measures approximately 41" (104 cm) from beginning ch, ending by working a White **right** side row; do **not** change color.

Finish off leaving a long end for sewing. Cut Mint and Red.

With **right** side together, matching sts on last row with beginning ch, whipstitch seam *(Fig. 6, page 59)*.

First Side Trim

With **right** side facing, working around carried colors **and** around dc at end of rows, join Mint with sc in last White row worked *(see Joining With Sc, page 58)*; 7 dc in next row, (sc in next row, 7 dc in next row) around; skip Row 1 and join with slip st to first sc, finish off.

Second Side Trim

With **right** side facing, working around carried colors **and** around dc at end of rows, join Mint with sc in Row 2; 7 dc in next row, (sc in next row, 7 dc in next row) around; skip Row 1 and join with slip st to first sc, finish off.

Triangle Mesh

BASIC

Shopping List

Yarn (Super Bulky Weight)

[3.5 ounces, 89 yards (100 grams, 81 meters) per skein]:

- ☐ 2 skeins

Crochet Hook

- ☐ Size M/N (9 mm) **or** size needed for gauge

Additional Supplies

- ☐ Yarn needle

Finished Size: 10¾" wide x 63¾" circumference (27.5 cm x 162 cm)

GAUGE INFORMATION

In pattern, one repeat = 3½" (9 cm); 4 rows = 5" (12.75 cm)

Gauge Swatch: 10¾" wide x 5" high (27.5 cm x 12.75 cm)

Work same as Cowl for 4 rows: 7 sts and 6 ch-3 sps.

STITCH GUIDE

TREBLE CROCHET ***(abbreviated tr)***

YO twice, insert hook in st indicated, YO and pull up a loop (4 loops on hook), (YO and draw through 2 loops on hook) 3 times.

COWL

Ch 25.

Row 1 (Right side)**:** Sc in tenth ch from hook, ch 3, skip next 2 chs, tr in next ch, ★ ch 3, skip next 2 chs, sc in next ch, ch 3, skip next 2 chs, tr in next ch; repeat from ★ once **more**: 7 sts and 6 sps.

Note: Loop a short piece of yarn around any stitch to mark Row 1 as **right** side.

Row 2: Ch 1, turn; sc in first tr, ch 2, skip next ch-3 sp, tr in next sc, ch 2, ★ skip next ch-3 sp, sc in next tr, ch 2, skip next ch-3 sp, tr in next sc, ch 2; repeat from ★ once **more**, skip next 3 chs, sc in next ch.

Row 3: Ch 7, turn; skip next ch-2 sp, sc in next tr, ch 3, skip next ch-2 sp, tr in next sc, ★ ch 3, skip next ch-2 sp, sc in next tr, ch 3, skip next ch-2 sp, tr in next sc; repeat from ★ across.

Rows 4-51: Repeat Rows 2 and 3, 24 times; at end of Row 51, finish off leaving a long end for sewing.

With **right** side together, matching sts on last row with beginning ch, whipstitch seam ***(Fig. 6, page 59)***.

Fringe

Beginning in Row 3, add fringe in top of tr every fourth row on each side of Cowl as follows:

Cut a piece of cardboard 3" (7.5 cm) wide by 5" (12.5 cm) high. Wind the yarn **loosely** and **evenly** lengthwise around the cardboard until the card is filled, then cut across one end; repeat as needed.

Hold together 2 strands of yarn; fold in half.

With **wrong** side of Cowl facing and using a crochet hook, draw the folded end up through the stitch indicated and pull the loose ends through the folded end ***(Fig. A)***; draw the knot up **tightly** ***(Fig. B)***. Repeat, spacing as indicated.

Trim ends if desired.

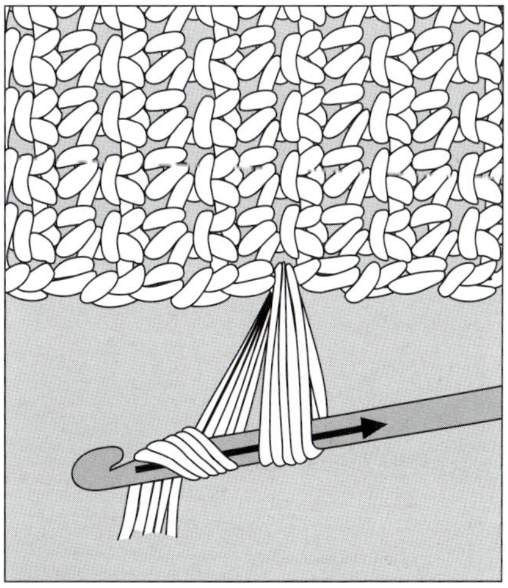

Fig. A

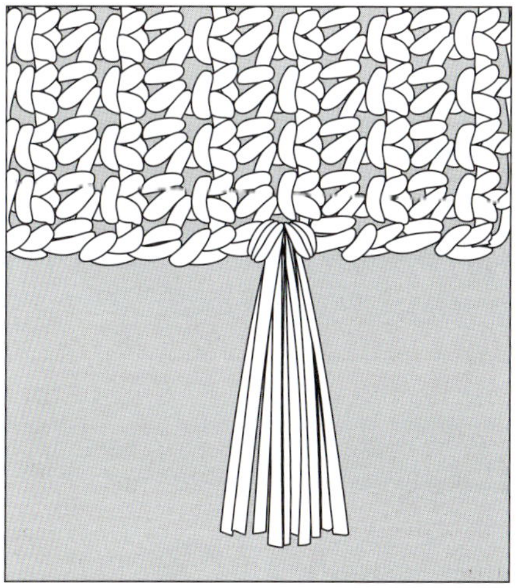

Fig. B

Ribbed

BASIC

Shopping List

Yarn (Medium Weight)

[5 ounces, 223 yards
(141 grams, 204 meters)
per skein]:

☐ 1 skein

Crochet Hook

☐ Size H (5 mm)
or size needed for gauge

Additional Supplies

☐ Yarn needle

Finished Size:
5¼" wide x 25" circumference
(13.5 cm x 63.5 cm)

GAUGE INFORMATION

In pattern,
16 sts and 9 rows = 4" (10 cm)

Gauge Swatch: 4" (10 cm) square
Ch 18.
Work same as Cowl for 9 rows: 16 sts.
Finish off.

STITCH GUIDE

FRONT POST DOUBLE CROCHET ***(abbreviated FPdc)***
YO, insert hook from **front** to **back** around post of st indicated ***(Fig. 4, page 58)***, YO and pull up a loop (3 loops on hook), (YO and draw through 2 loops on hook) twice.

BACK POST DOUBLE CROCHET ***(abbreviated BPdc)***
YO, insert hook from **back** to **front** around post of st indicated ***(Fig. 4, page 58)***, YO and pull up a loop (3 loops on hook), (YO and draw through 2 loops on hook) twice.

COWL

Ch 102.

Row 1: Dc in third ch from hook and in each ch across: 100 dc.

Row 2 (Right side)**:** Ch 2 (does **not** count as a st), turn; work FPdc around each of first 2 dc, work BPdc around each of next 2 dc, ★ work FPdc around each of next 2 dc, work BPdc around each of next 2 dc; repeat from ★ across.

Note: Loop a short piece of yarn around any stitch to mark Row 2 as **right** side.

Row 3: Ch 2, turn; work FPdc around each of first 2 sts, work BPdc around each of next 2 sts, ★ work FPdc around each of next 2 sts, work BPdc around each of next 2 sts; repeat from ★ across.

Repeat Row 3 for pattern until piece measures approximately 5¼" (13.5 cm) from beginning ch, ending by working a **right** side row.

Finish off leaving a long end for sewing.

With **right** side facing, sew ends of rows together using mattress stitch ***(Figs. 5a & b, page 59)***.

Green Tea & Velvet

BASIC

Shopping List

Yarn (Medium Weight)

MEDIUM 4

[3.5 ounces, 186 yards
(100 grams, 170 meters)
per skein]:

- ☐ Dk Green - 2 skeins
- ☐ Lime - 1 skein

Crochet Hook

- ☐ Size I (5.5 mm)
  or size needed for gauge

Additional Supplies

- ☐ Yarn needle

Finished Size:
10" wide x 39" circumference
(25.5 cm x 99 cm)

GAUGE INFORMATION

In pattern,
14 sc = 4" (10 cm);
16 rows = 4¼" (10.75 cm)
Rows 1-11 = 3" (7.5 cm)

Gauge Swatch: 7½" wide x 3" high
(19 cm x 7.5 cm)

Work same as Cowl for 11 rows: 18 sc and 8 FPtr.

STITCH GUIDE

FRONT POST TREBLE CROCHET
(abbreviated FPtr)

YO twice, insert hook from **front** to **back** around post of sc indicated *(Fig. 4, page 58)*, YO and pull up a loop (4 loops on hook), (YO and draw through 2 loops on hook) 3 times.

COWL

With Dk Green, ch 27.

Row 1 (Right side)**:** Sc in second ch from hook, dc in next ch, (sc in next ch, dc in next ch) across changing to Lime in last dc *(Fig. 2b, page 58)*; cut Dk Green: 26 sts.

Note: Loop a short piece of yarn around any stitch to mark Row 1 as **right** side.

Row 2: Ch 1, turn; sc in first dc, dc in next sc, (sc in next dc, dc in next sc) across changing to Dk Green in last dc, cut Lime.

Row 3: Ch 1, turn; sc in first dc, dc in next sc, (sc in next dc, dc in next sc) across changing to Lime in last dc, cut Dk Green.

Rows 4-6: Ch 1, turn; sc in each st across.

Row 7: Ch 1, turn; sc in first 3 sc, work FPtr around first sc 3 rows **below**, skip next 4 sc, work FPtr around next sc, ★ skip next 2 sc from last sc worked on **previous** row, sc in next 4 sc, work FPtr around next sc 3 rows **below**, skip next 4 sc, work FPtr around next sc; repeat from ★ 2 times **more**, skip next 2 sc from last sc worked on **previous** row, sc in last 3 sc: 18 sc and 8 FPtr.

Rows 8-10: Ch 1, turn; sc in each st across: 26 sc.

Row 11: Ch 1, turn; sc in first sc, work FPtr around fourth sc 3 rows **below**, skip next sc from last sc worked on **previous** row, sc in next 4 sc, work FPtr around next sc 3 rows **below**, ★ skip next 4 sc, work FPtr around next sc, skip next 2 sc from last sc worked on **previous** row, sc in next 4 sc, work FPtr around next sc 3 rows **below**; repeat from ★ 2 times **more**, skip next sc from last sc worked on **previous** row, sc in last sc changing to Dk Green *(Fig. 2a, page 58)*, cut Lime: 18 sc and 8 FPtr.

Rows 12-19: Repeat Rows 4-11, changing to Lime at end of last row, cut Dk Green.

Rows 20-139: Repeat Rows 4-19, 7 times; then repeat Rows 4-11 once **more**.

Row 140: Ch 1, turn; sc in first st, dc in next st, (sc in next st, dc in next st) across changing to Lime in last dc, cut Dk Green.

Row 141: Ch 1, turn; sc in first dc, dc in next sc, (sc in next dc, dc in next sc) across changing to Dk Green in last dc, cut Lime.

Row 142: Ch 1, turn; sc in first dc, dc in next sc, (sc in next dc, dc in next sc) across; finish off.

Trim

Row 1: With **wrong** side of one long edge facing and working in ends of rows, join Dk Green with sc in first row ***(see Joining With Sc, page 58)***; work an odd number of sc evenly across.

Row 2 (Right side)**:** Ch 1, turn; sc in first sc, (dc in next sc, sc in next sc) across changing to Lime in last sc, cut Dk Green.

Row 3: Ch 3 **(counts as first dc)**, turn; (sc in next dc, dc in next sc) across changing to Dk Green in last dc; cut Lime.

Row 4: Ch 1, turn; sc in first dc, (dc in next sc, sc in next dc) across.

Row 5: Ch 1, do **not** turn; working from **left** to **right**, work reverse sc in each st across ***(Figs. 7a-d, page 59)***; finish off.

Repeat Trim across opposite long edge; at end of Row 5, finish off leaving a long end for sewing.

With **right** side together, matching sts on last row with beginning ch and ends of rows of Trim, whipstitch seam ***(Fig. 6, page 59)***.

General Instructions

ABBREVIATIONS

BPdc	Back Post double crochet(s)
ch(s)	chain(s)
cm	centimeters
dc	double crochet(s)
dc3tog	double crochet 3 together
FPdc	Front Post double crochet(s)
FPtr	Front Post treble crochet(s)
hdc	half double crochet(s)
mm	millimeters
sc	single crochet(s)
sp(s)	space(s)
st(s)	stitch(es)
tr	treble crochet(s)
YO	yarn over

UNITED STATES		INTERNATIONAL
slip stitch (slip st)	=	single crochet (sc)
single crochet (sc)	=	double crochet (dc)
half double crochet (hdc)	=	half treble crochet (htr)
double crochet (dc)	=	treble crochet (tr)
treble crochet (tr)	=	double treble crochet (dtr)
double treble crochet (dtr)	=	triple treble crochet (ttr)
triple treble crochet (tr tr)	=	quadruple treble crochet (qtr)
skip	=	miss

SYMBOLS & TERMS

★ — work instructions following ★ as many **more** times as indicated in addition to the first time.

( ) or [ ] — work the enclosed instructions **as many** times as specified by the number immediately following **or** work all enclosed instructions in stitch or space indicated **or** contains explanatory remarks.

colon — the number(s) given after a colon at the end of a row denote(s) the number of stitches or spaces you should have on that row.

Yarn Weight Symbol & Names	LACE 0	SUPER FINE 1	FINE 2	LIGHT 3	MEDIUM 4	BULKY 5	SUPER BULKY 6	JUMBO 7
Type of Yarns in Category	Fingering, size 10 crochet thread	Sock, Fingering, Baby	Sport, Baby	DK, Light Worsted	Worsted, Afghan, Aran	Chunky, Craft, Rug	Super Bulky, Roving	Jumbo, Roving
Crochet Gauge* Ranges in Single Crochet to 4" (10 cm)	32-42 sts**	21-32 sts	16-20 sts	12-17 sts	11-14 sts	8-11 sts	6-9 sts	5 sts and fewer
Advised Hook Size Range	Steel*** 6 to 8, Regular hook B-1	B-1 to E-4	E-4 to 7	7 to I-9	I-9 to K-10½	K-10½ to M/N-13	M/N-13 to Q	Q and larger

*GUIDELINES ONLY: The chart above reflects the most commonly used gauges and hook sizes for specific yarn categories.

** Lace weight yarns are usually crocheted with larger hooks to create lacy openwork patterns. Accordingly, a gauge range is difficult to determine. Always follow the gauge stated in your pattern.

*** Steel crochet hooks are sized differently from regular hooks–the higher the number, the smaller the hook, which is the reverse of regular hook sizing.

BASIC	Projects using basic stitches. May include basic increases and decreases.
EASY	Projects may include simple stitch patterns, color work, and/or shaping.
INTERMEDIATE	Projects may include involved stitch patterns, color work, and/or shaping.
COMPLEX	Projects may include complex stitch patterns, color work, and/or shaping using a variety of techniques and stitches simultaneously.

CROCHET HOOKS																	
U.S.	B-1	C-2	D-3	E-4	F-5	G-6	7	H-8	I-9	J-10	K-10½	L-11	M/N-13	N/P-15	P/Q	Q	S
Metric - mm	2.25	2.75	3.25	3.5	3.75	4	4.5	5	5.5	6	6.5	8	9	10	15	16	19

GAUGE

Exact gauge is **essential** for proper size. Before beginning your project, make the sample swatch given in the individual instructions in the yarn and hook specified. After completing the swatch, measure it, counting your stitches and rows carefully. If your swatch is larger or smaller than specified, **make another, changing the hook size to get the correct gauge.** Keep trying until you find the size that will give you the specified gauge.

JOINING WITH SC

When instructed to join with sc, begin with a slip knot on hook. Insert hook in stitch or space indicated, YO and pull up a loop, YO and draw through both loops on hook.

BACK OR FRONT LOOP ONLY

Work only in loop(s) indicated by arrow ***(Fig. 1)***.

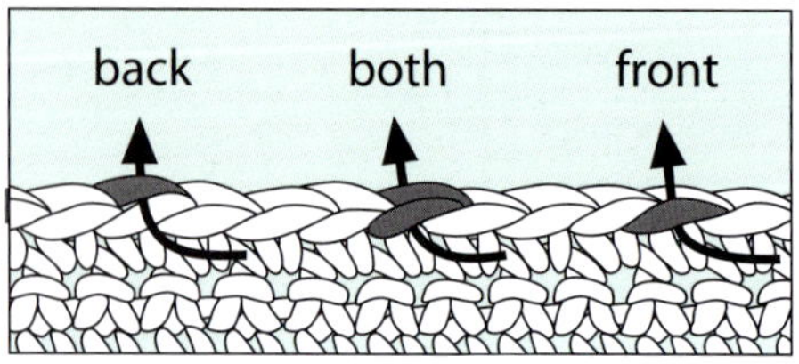

Fig. 1

CHANGING COLORS

Work the last stitch to within one step of completion, hook new yarn ***(Fig. 2a or Fig. 2b)*** and draw through both loops on hook.

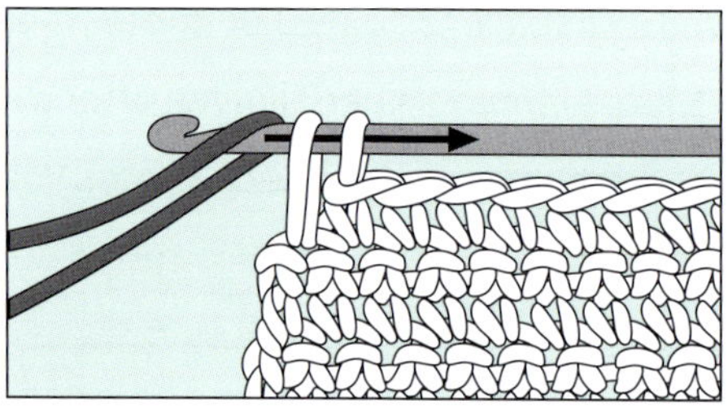

Fig. 2a

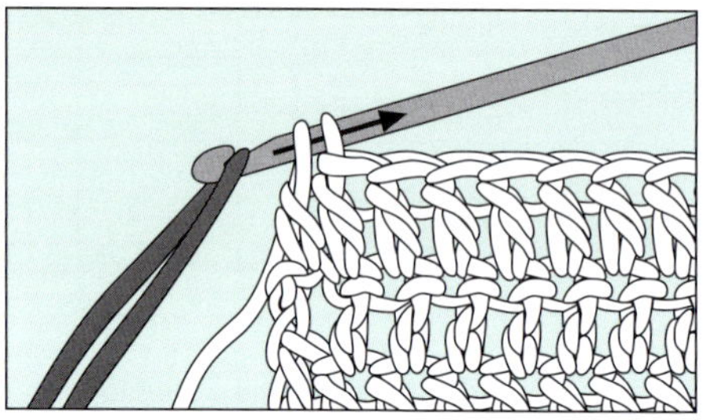

Fig. 2b

WORKING IN SPACE BEFORE A STITCH

When instructed to work in space **before** a stitch or in spaces **between** stitches, insert hook in space indicated by arrow ***(Fig. 3)***.

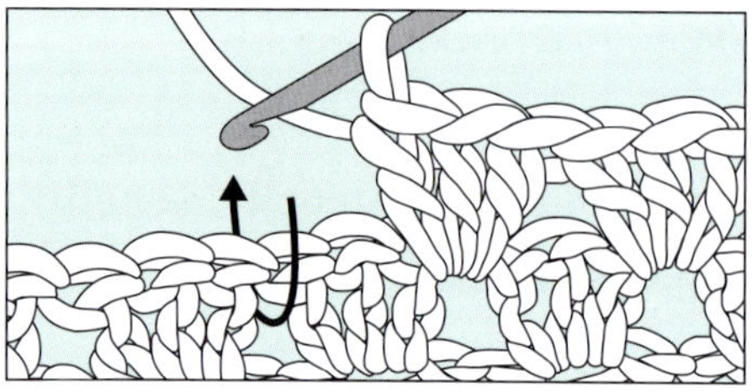

Fig. 3

POST STITCH

Work around post of stitch indicated, inserting hook in direction of arrow ***(Fig. 4)***.

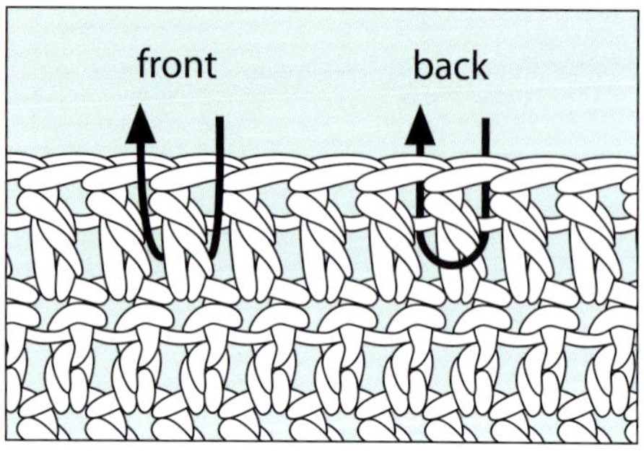

Fig. 4

MATTRESS STITCH

With **right** side of both edges facing you and matching rows, sew through both sides once to secure the seam. Insert the needle from **back** to **front** through two strands on one side ***(Fig. 5a)***, then from **back** to **front** on the other side ***(Fig. 5b)***. Continue in this manner drawing the seam together as you work. This will create a flat seam.

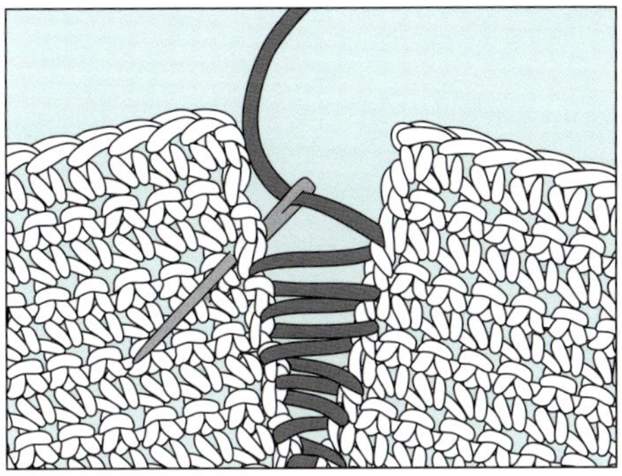

Fig. 5a

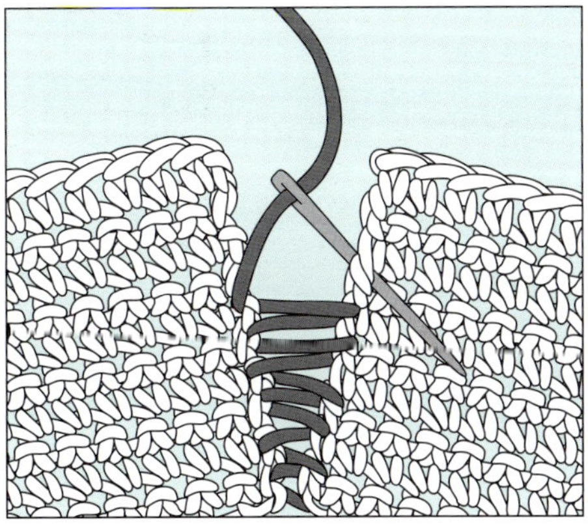

Fig. 5b

WHIPSTITCH

With **right** side together, sew through stitches on both sides once to secure the beginning of the seam. Insert the needle from **front** to **back** through **both** loops on **both** sides ***(Fig. 6)***. Bring the needle around and insert it from **front** to **back** through next loops of both sides. Continue in this manner across, keeping the sewing yarn fairly loose.

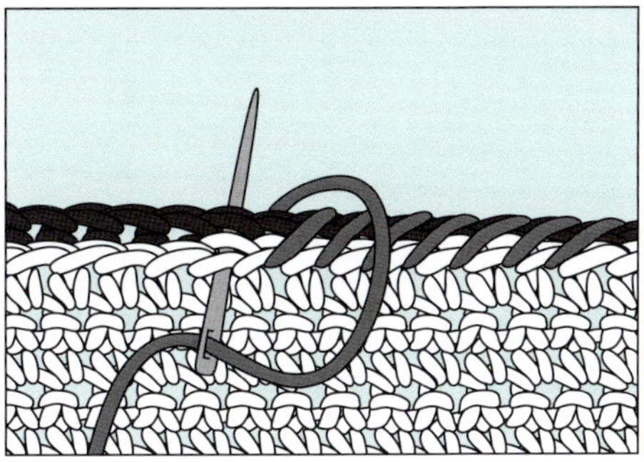

Fig. 6

REVERSE SINGLE CROCHET

Working from **left** to **right**, ★ insert hook in stitch or end of row to right of hook ***(Fig. 7a)***, YO and draw through, under and to left of loop on hook (2 loops on hook) ***(Fig. 7b)***, YO and draw through both loops on hook ***(Fig. 7c)*** **(reverse sc made, *Fig. 7d*)**; repeat from ★ around.

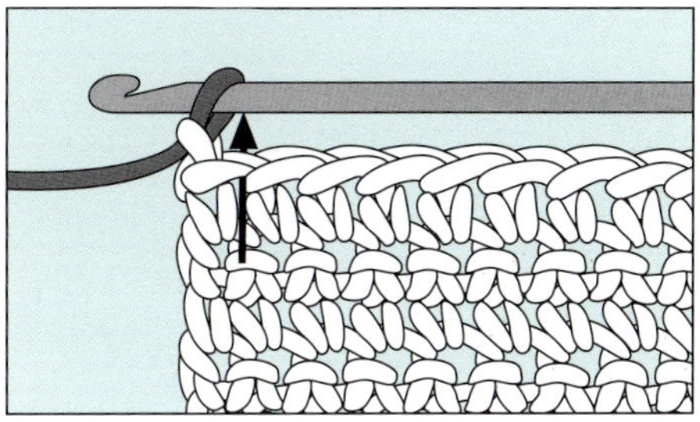

Fig. 7a

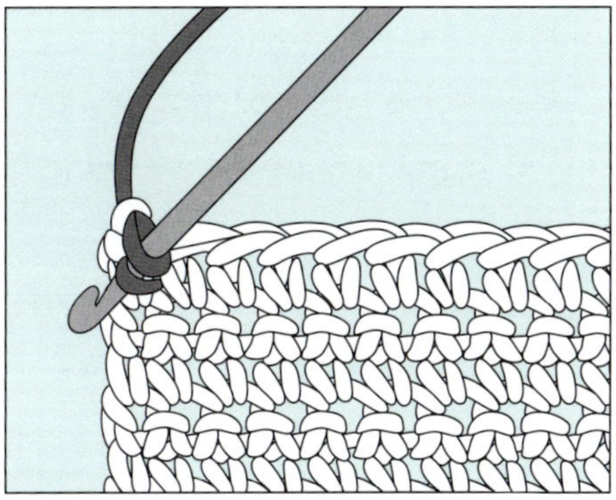

Fig. 7b

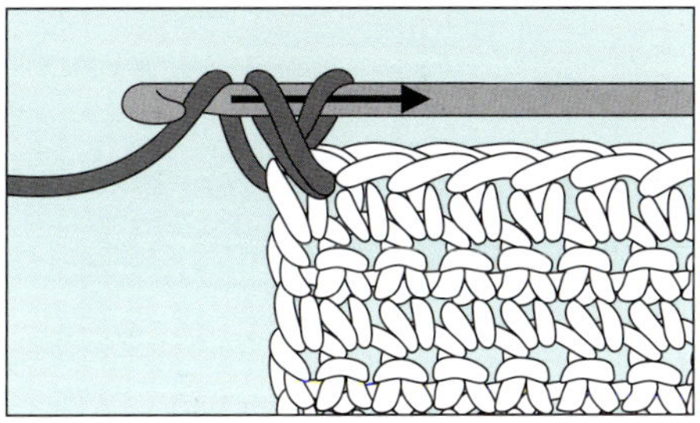

Fig. 7c

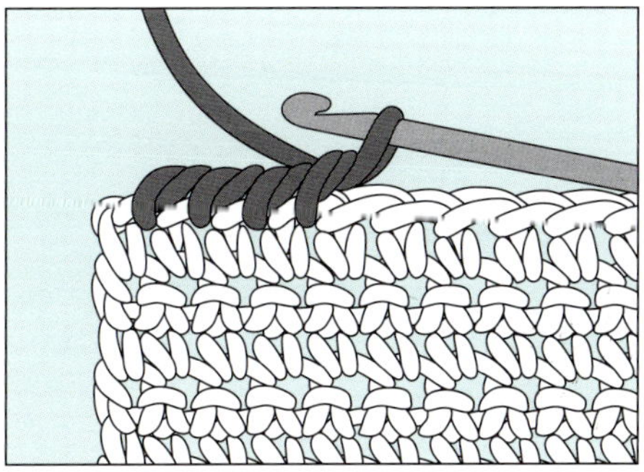

Fig. 7d

Basic Crochet Stitches

CHAIN

To work a chain stitch, begin with a slip knot on the hook. Bring the yarn **over** hook from **back** to **front**, catching the yarn with the hook and turning the hook slightly toward you to keep the yarn from slipping off. Draw the yarn through the slip knot ***(Fig. 8)*** **(first chain st made, *abbreviated ch*)**.

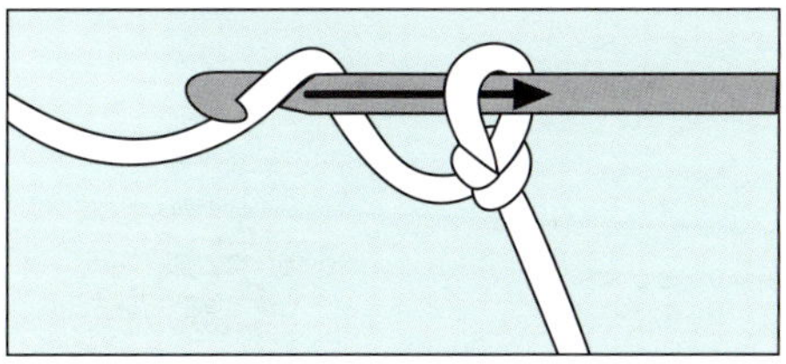

Fig. 8

WORKING INTO THE CHAIN

Method 1: Insert hook into back ridge of each chain ***(Fig. 9a)***.

Method 2: Insert hook under top two strands of each chain ***(Fig. 9b)***.

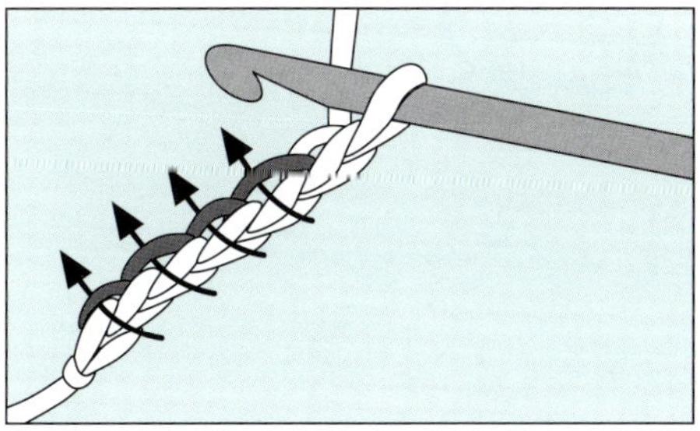

Fig. 9a

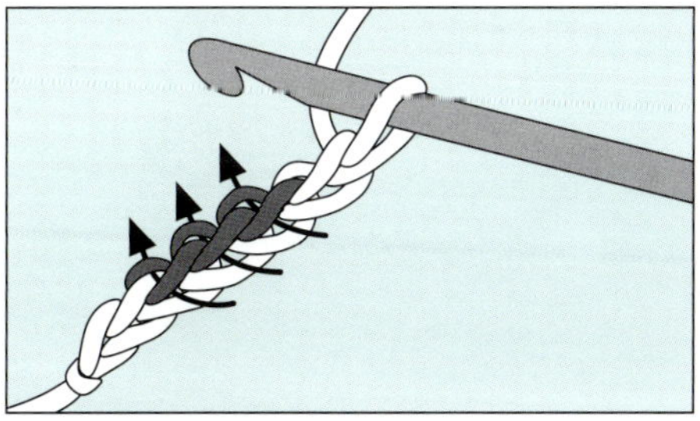

Fig. 9b

SLIP STITCH

To work a slip stitch, insert hook in stitch indicated, YO and draw through st and through loop on hook ***(Fig. 10)*** **(slip stitch made, *abbreviated slip st*)**.

Fig. 10

SINGLE CROCHET

Insert hook in stitch indicated, YO and pull up a loop, YO and draw through both loops on hook ***(Fig. 11)*** **(single crochet made, *abbreviated sc*)**.

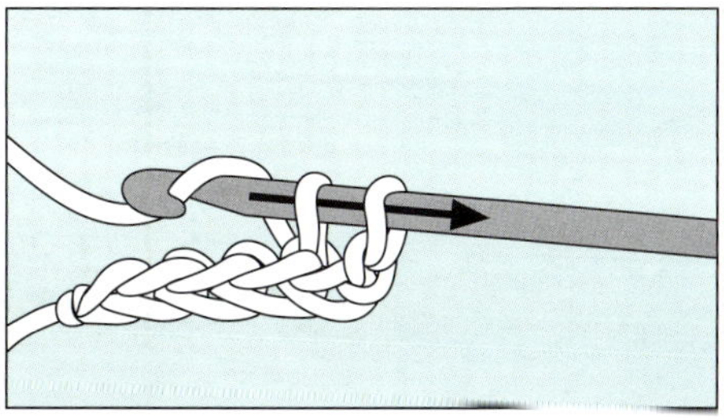

Fig. 11

HALF DOUBLE CROCHET

YO, insert hook in stitch indicated, YO and pull up a loop, YO and draw through all 3 loops on hook ***(Fig. 12)*** **(half double crochet made, *abbreviated hdc*)**.

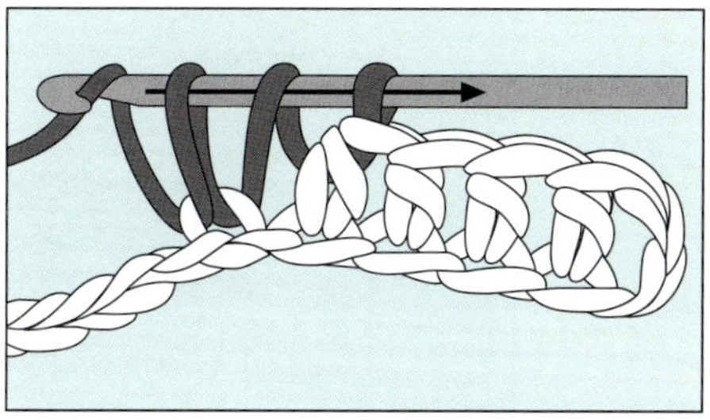

Fig. 12

DOUBLE CROCHET

YO, insert hook in stitch indicated, YO and pull up a loop (3 loops on hook), YO and draw through 2 loops on hook ***(Fig. 13a)***, YO and draw through remaining 2 loops on hook ***(Fig. 13b)*** **(double crochet made, *abbreviated dc*)**.

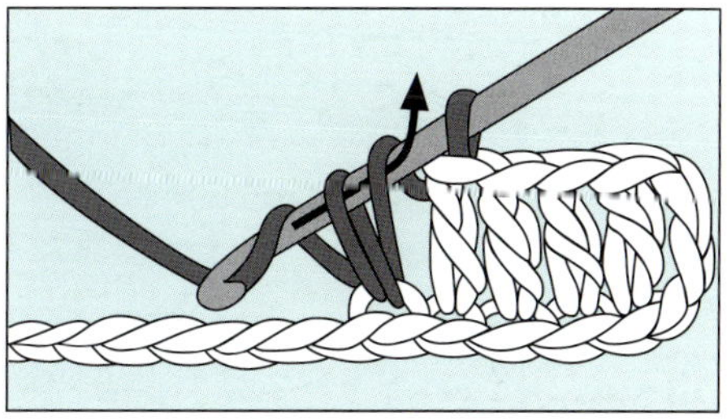

Fig. 13a

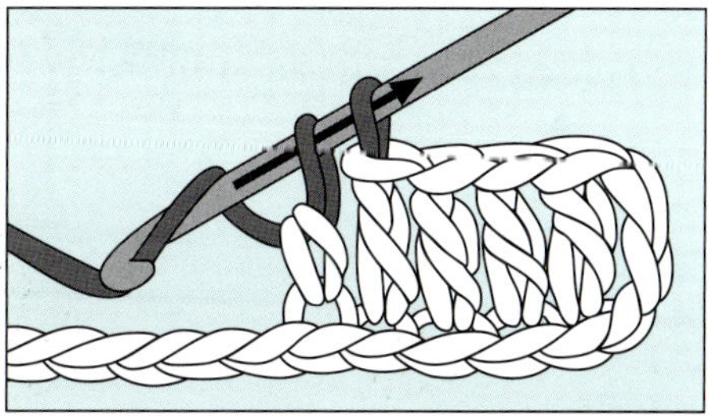

Fig. 13b

TREBLE CROCHET

YO twice, insert hook in stitch indicated, YO and pull up a loop (4 loops on hook), (YO and draw through 2 loops on hook) 3 times ***(Figs. 14a-c)*** **(treble crochet made, *abbreviated tr*)**.

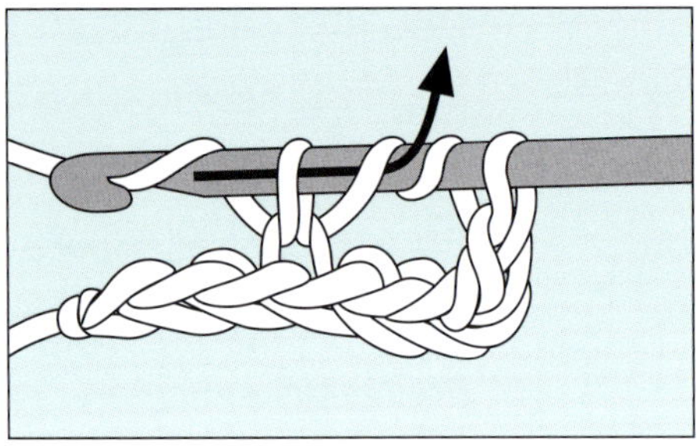

Fig. 14a

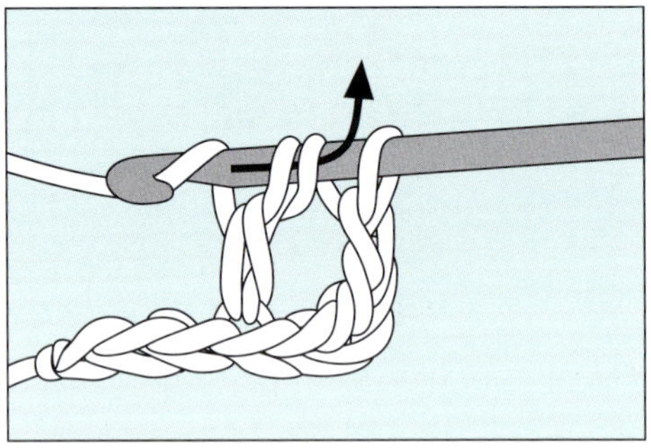

Fig. 14b

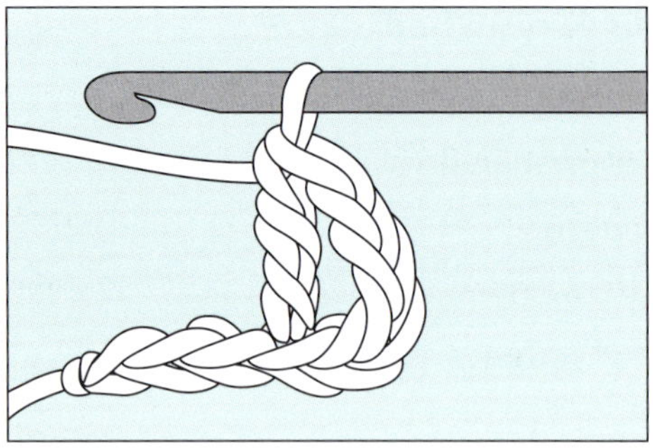

Fig. 14c

Yarn Information

The Cowls in this book were made using various weights of yarn. Any brand of the specified yarn weight may be used. It is best to refer to the yardage/meters when determining how many balls or skeins to purchase. Remember, to arrive at the finished size, it is the GAUGE/ TENSION that is important, not the brand of yarn.

For your convenience, the specific yarns used to create our photography models are listed. Because yarn manufacturers make frequent changes in their product lines, you may sometimes find it necessary to use a substitute yarn or to search for the discontinued product at alternate suppliers (locally or online).

LINEN STITCH
Red Heart® Hopscotch™
#7950 Scooter

CHEVRON
Red Heart® Super Saver Ombré™
#3961 Scuba

LINEN & V-STITCHES
Red Heart® Chic Sheep by Marly Bird™
#5254 Sunset

COLOR BLOCK FILET
Red Heart® Soft®
Grey - #9010 Charcoal
White - #4600 White
Green - #9870 Deep Sea
Lt Grey - #9440 Lt Grey Heather

DREAMY
Red Heart® Dreamy™
#8341 Grey

BLUE LACE
Red Heart® Chic Sheep by Marly Bird™
#5687 VIP

CHIC CHEVRON
Red Heart® Chic Sheep by Marly Bird™
Mint - #5635 Crème de Mint
White - #5311 Lace
Red - #5254 Sunset

TRIANGLE MESH
Red Heart® Evermore™
#9933 Cotton Candy

RIBBED
Red Heart® With Love Stripes™
#1975 Sandbar Stripe

GREEN TEA & VELVET
Red Heart® Chic Sheep by Marly Bird™
Dk Green - #5633 Velvet
Lime - #5620 Green Tea

We have made every effort to ensure that these instructions are accurate and complete. We cannot, however, be responsible for human error, typographical mistakes, or variations in individual work.

Production Team: Instructional/Technical Editors - Linda A. Daley and Lois J. Long; Senior Graphic Artist - Lora Puls; Graphic Artist - Lori S. Malkin; Photo Stylist - Lori Wenger; and Photographer - Jason Masters.

Library of Congress Control Number: 2018957905

Made in U.S.A.